THE DEATHBED

AFTERLIFE

KISHAN MOHAN ANKOLEKAR

ISBN 979-888503725-9

I would dedicate this book to my parents.

Contents

Foreword

I would like to thank the life

Preface

Journey of life

Acknowledgements

I would acknowledge the books

Prologue

Thank you

Fade

Gone are the days when sparrow dwelled a Vignette

Gone are the days when grandma pickled a marinate

Gone are the days when wriggler was used as a bait

Gone are the days when cuprous was used as a plate

Gone are the days when rhymes bumped a plait

Gone are the days when artisan expressed the innate

Gone are the days when plundered mango and tamarin filled a pocket

Gone are the days when letter made a heart deflate

Walking the Autumn

Torrent breezes are blowing the mist

Concealed on blooming floret

As if telling me, the autumn has ensued

To blow of my suffering Koret

Squawking squirrels on the wood seems

Toddler behaving like Morret

Chirping sparrows with their brood

Seems enquiring about my sonnet

Singing cuckoo with its voice in a shroud

Seems inviting me to join its duet

As if telling the autumn has ensued

To blow of my sorrowful coffret

Afterlife

Here am I in heaven or hell don't know

But I can say that almighty foreknow

I was in ellipsoid making a living

Passaging through life by wondering and smiling

I am grateful for the beautiful life I lead

But I was in sorrow when I was in my last bed

I am feeling this place dark and Blake

Cannot hear and see bird and lake

I can see the beautiful fairy on the cloud

But I am in sorrow where are my blood and beloved

Hornbill call

O thunder, o Rain

I call honor thy harvest thy nature

Descend thy sky thy mountain

Perceive thy fish thy figs

Whiff thy floret thy earth

Heed thy aphis thy avian

O thunder, O rain

I call honor thy harvest thy nature

Siberian crane

I Siberian crane voyaging from Russ

Passing through frozen arctic spruce

I can see the Altai mountains in the pellucid

Waters Of lake Baikal

And Vasyugan meandering in Tomsk Oblast

I was sacred in the tribes of Yakuts and Yukaghir

Also, Ustad Mansur revered me in the court of Jahangir

I am in despair my antecedent has vanished from Bharatpur

But there is a glimmer of hope for my brairn in Nagpur

Culture

The sound of brass resonating in the air

The fragrance of jasmine unfurling the streets

Escalating the enthusiasm of the occasion

reverberating mantras scouring the stains of evil

sitar, Veena, Nadaswaram, Ghatam vanquishing the clamor of folks

the aroma of damar Batu flaring the divinity

Goddess Durga clad with silk saree embellished with jewelry charming its devotees with her beauty and might

Dasara

**Mandapa unfurled with blossom
Resembling the crimson sunlight
Luminescence of palace making the dead
of the night bright
Tribe fervouring the night to capture
Alluring deity sight
Rumble of tusker demolishing the
Tranquility of night
Mysore Pak, Huli thavve relinquishing
The devotee's appetite
A beautiful Channapatna toy making a
Innocent toddlers fight
This is the sight of the foremost night**

9 798885 037259

Printed by Libri Plureos GmbH in Hamburg,
Germany